Ten Steps to Fast Cash from Home

Tried and Tested; easy methods to pull in extra money

J. Goldenberg
E. McNew
COPYRIGHT © 2014
First Printing March 22, 2014

Houston, TX
Printed in the USA

CONTENS

Disclaimer

This narrative is written to offer information and education to our readers. It is sold/uploaded with the understanding that the publisher and/or author is not engaged to render any type of psychological, legal, or any other kind of professional advice. This content is the sole expression and opinion of the author. Neither the publisher nor the individual author(s) shall be liable for any physical, psychological, emotional, financial, or commercial damages, including, but not limited to, special, incidental, consequential or other damages. Our views and rights are the same: You are responsible for your own choices, actions, and results.

I would like to expressly convey to you (the reader) that if I were to accidentally defame, purge, humiliate and/or hurt someone's person or feelings as a result of reading and/or acting upon any or all of the information and/or advice found in my content, it is entirely unintentional of me to do so.

By continuing to read and interpret the remainder of this guide, *Ten Steps to Fast Cash from Home,* written by J. Goldenberg, you are waiving any rights to sue in court of law myself and/or any other person involved with this narrative in any way. I, J. Goldenberg, shall not be held responsible for any physical, emotional, or other damages. If you, the reader, find any of my content to be insulting, malicious, insensitive, or unnecessary, contact me at **mcnewpublishing@gmail.com** so I may rectify the problem.

Introduction

Most all of us are searching for a way to lift the financial burdens off of our shoulders in one way or another. Most all of us also don't know that it is very possible to work online, and eventually generate enough revenue to have the option to make this our *main* source of income. And if we do know this, we are still confused and lost for the sources. I am not going to leave you hanging with "affiliate" programs or surveys. These can make money, but they take a ton of time and patience, and can cause some quick frustration.

This guide is not going to offer you *more* information. This guide is going to offer you the *right* information. You may or may not have heard of some of the sources I will reveal in the following chapters. Regardless, this guide is going to offer you *much more* than a website.

This guide will offer valuable information, and I will reveal the following:

Who can work for these sources?

What is the job made up of?

How much money can you make?

Why is this a reliable source of income?

The point where we get confused, is when there are so many different online competitors desperate to find people to become affiliates, sellers, or customers; that it all turns into one big storm of online competition, which then become difficult to trust and differentiate from. In my first book, My Secret List of Sites that Pay, I mention very quickly that if any online business requests for you to pay them anything, in any amount, before YOU start working for THEM, it's a huge RED FLAG. If this happens, stop in your tracks and click on that X icon.

I have personally tested every outlet listed in this book, and I have been able to comfortably work solely from home for the last two years. Before we get started, you will need to keep in mind that it will take work, trial and error, a will to succeed, and a good effort on your part to get the ball rolling. Nothing good will ever come free, but the effort will be well worth it. These resources usually pay out pretty quickly, ranging from instant PayPal transfers to payments every month. I have listed ten steps, with the first two reflecting on a personal level. This is so you can not only make money from home, but actually enjoy what you are doing as well.

The reason I have these paying websites/employment opportunities listed as a step-method is simple. If you follow through with all of these steps, even if you're not interested (step out of that comfort zone!), you are bound to find at least ONE source of online income, and hopefully more, that you are happy to continue with.

Let's go!

Step one

First and foremost, before you even start *thinking* about working online, you must ask yourself some questions. Grab a pen and notepad, and write your answers down. It's truly amazing what writing and re-reading can teach you about yourself!

How strong is your desire?

To what lengths are you willing to go to be financially independent and work on your own time? Every person who ever turned out successful (at age twenty or ninety!) had the desire. They were willing to go to whatever extent necessary to meet their goal(s), and even after several failures, they still got back up and kept pushing. Are you willing to stay persistent and climb that ladder even if you stumble a few times? If not, why?

What are your Intentions?

Why do you want to work online? Money? More time with family? Meeting new contacts? Education? Helping other people? If your goal is purely money, you will need to keep in mind that building a strategic set of goals is a must. It's all a learning process, and you won't get rich over-night.

Are your expectations realistic?

Do you plan on slowly easing into the online world of money-making, while you stay with your regular job? Do you plan on going full-force and quitting your job, the first time you get a paycheck? Do you have a savings built up to allow you time off of work while you integrate into the internet biz? Plan accordingly. You could begin making tons of money in the first month, or it could take you six months.

How much time are you willing to invest?

Depending on which avenue you take online, some income sources can require extensive knowledge and/or time. Are you willing to take that time, even if it means working *after* your regular job, to learn the ropes, experiment with trial/error, and face possible set-backs along the way?

*Now go back and read your answers. The point of this exercise is to determine if you're all-in, or simply looking for a quick financial remedy. If you are not 110% sure that you are ready to commit and invest yourself into running your own business, or simply working from home, don't make plans to leave your job just yet. I can't guarantee that you will make money instantly. However, if you stick to it, figure out exactly what you want, and work hard, you will be rewarded! If you are going to succeed financially, be ready to commit and devote your life!

Step Two

Now that we've determined what your expectations are for working for yourself, we have a few more things to consider. *Very important* things. How can we get the best out of this life-changing experience, and get you working in an area that you love? Remember, money is great, but it does not make a person 100% happy. These two questions below are very important. Read through them and really think about what is being asked. If you can apply these concepts to your online career, you will be much more successful!

What am I good at? What are my talents?

What are the two most common compliments that you receive from others? Are you a good listener? Quick learner? Are you an expert in something? What do you think you're good at? What do you want to be good at?

What is my passion?

If you're not quite sure, that's ok. We all have our own definition of "passion". I break it down in this yahoo article here. Your passion can't be something that you consciously seek out. This is because it's natural, and has been natural to you for your entire life. Some people never find their passion. It took me until I was twenty-six to discover mine. This is because I did not believe that I truly loved to write, despite others constantly sending me compliments. I wanted to be something way better than a writer when I grew up. I stopped writing for about five years, and when I picked up again, good things began to happen. The universe was working with me, and for me, because I was meant to write.

Finding your passion involves taking risks. We need to step outside of our comfort zone, and try anything and everything that we never thought we'd try. When you find your passion, you will know it with a thousand percent certainty.

*These questions are important for a couple of reasons. First, if we can recognize our talents, and what we excel in, we can apply this to any work we do and see great results. Second, if you have found your passion, you will also be able to apply this to any work you do, but you will be taken to many, many more opportunities along the way. When you are passionate and excited about something, it reflects off of you, and others naturally sense what you were put on the planet to do.

If you still just don't know, you'll get there. Remember to try new things, take risks, and let it come naturally.

Let's start applying our unique strengths, and make some money!

Step Three

www.leapforce.com

Who can work for Leapforce?

You must be at least 18 years old, and you must take a three part exam and successfully pass. Leapforce will send you the material to study about a week in advance, after you send them your personal information and quick application. The test is a challenge, but I believe that anyone can pass the exam if they *really* study. If you do not pass the first time, leapforce will usually allow you to re-take the test one additional time. It covers the basics of the job you will be doing, what to-do, not-do-do, and the general guidelines.

What the job is made up of?

Once hired, you will become a Leapforce independent contractor. You will be evaluating search engines for Leapforce clients. This is pretty much rating the websites on the search engines, which helps determine their relevance and rank to the search term. Although not a stipulation to my knowledge, Leapforce will ask you if you are comfortable with possibly having to view explicit material once in a while. It just depends on the task in which you are assigned. Unfortunately, those dirty websites have to be put in the rank system too. My opinion with it was that I was just going to be professional and not let it get to me. It didn't come around all too often, either.

How much money can you make?

Leapforce generally starts their agents off at $13/hr. I've read that they do offer raises under certain circumstances, although I do not know exactly how much. This is a very decent pay- rate, for being able to work at home.

Why this is a reliable source of income?

It is consistent, and up to you as to how much your paycheck will be. If you have a family emergency come up, or just want to take a vacation and only get a few hours in for the week, they won't fire you, either. You will know exactly how much your next paycheck will be, because you chose your hours!

Step Four

Who can work for Lionbridge?

Lionbridge often looks for bilingual candidates with a strong interest in Internet-based communications and/or culture. This does not mean that you must have prior experience, or that you must be bilingual. Those are just favorable assets.

What is the job made up of?

Most positions are part-time, and work-from-home. The positions are flexible, ranging from IT to non-IT, to business processes, transaction processing, and online mapping services.

How much money can you make?

The pay is determined on employment. It also varies by country. Typically, Lionbridge will start their U.S. employees out at $14/hr.

Why is this a reliable source of income?

Although Lionbridge only pays out a maximum of 20 hours/week, just as with Leapforce, they are flexible and allow you to choose your own schedule. Your hours and pay are up to you!

I suggest trying both of these opportunities out, and see which better fits your professional and financial needs. Or, if you have extra time, try them both and see how you juggle.

Step Five

http://www.amazon.jobs/location/virtual-locations

Who can work for Amazon? (And I don't mean by selling your stuff!)

Once in a while, Amazon will have work-at-home positions available for anyone to apply to who meet the requirements.

What is the job made up of?

The work-at home jobs are made up of Customer Service Specialists, Administrative Support, Database Administration, Finance and Accounting, and Human Resources. Amazon hires temporary, freelancers, and full-time and part-time schedules. They also offer excellent benefits!

How much money can you make?

Amazon will usually start anywhere from $10-$14 per hour.

Why is this a reliable source of income?

Do I really have to answer this? It's Amazon! They're not going to stiff ya short!

And as the previous steps, you work as an independent contractor and know exactly what your schedule is. Now, because most of these jobs involve communicating with customers in one way or another, you will have to make sure that you develop some sort of a routing that is consistent. If you are scheduled to take calls and suddenly would rather zip yourself up into some footie-jammies and snack on Zebra Cakes, you might have some sort of repercussion.

Step Six

www.textbroker.com

Who can work for Textbroker?

Are you an entry-level to intermediate author, writer, freelancer, or blogger? If so, the answer is YOU!

What is the job made up of?

After submitting your personal information and an original content sample, you will be given a rating by the sites editors within a week. This rating determines the amount of articles you can be paid for. Depending on how many stars you are given, you will be paid X amount per/word of the article. The perks of this particular site is that as you progress, make money, and submit more articles, the editors are constantly rating them and giving you personalized advice on what you can do to improve your content, and essentially drive more sales.

How much money can you make?

This depends on the order type that the customer makes. You can make from 0.7 cents per word, to 5 cents per word if the order is open. If it's a "direct" or "team" order, you can choose your own price-per-word, regardless of your rating.

Why is this a reliable source of income?

As with many work-at-home jobs, this is also one which gives you the freedom to write as much, or as little as you like. This is a great way for any author to not only make extra money, but to improve their writing skills overall.

Step Seven

www.Applicants.usertesting.com

Who can work for Usertesting?

If you can pass their example test, you're good to go!

What is the job made up of?

This is a site that will pay you to test other customers' websites. When online businesses build their sites, they want to make sure that it is readable, easy to navigate and has a professional presentation before they launch it to the public. Usertesting will then send the request of the customer to one of the testers (you), and you simply go to the site and give it a good written and/or oral evaluation.

How much money can you make?

Currently, usertesting pays from $10-15 per site that you test. Based on the satisfaction of the customer, you will get a rating that can either increase or decrease more offers to test websites.

Why is this a reliable source of income?

The site has great ratings, they are reputable, and it's the perfect way to ease into the online market while still working at your regular job.

Step Eight

www.fiverr.com (I'll bet you've heard of this!)

Who can work for Fiverr?

Fiverr has users from all around the world, including buyers and sellers. Any person, with any skill or talent, or even the desire to simply make a fool of yourself...you're in!

What is the job made up of?

Whatever floats your boat! Seriously. Well, almost. This is where you will need to get creative, and ask yourself what you love doing best, what your passion is, and implement! I have a fiverr account, and my gigs are for review services and online marketing. It's easy, fun, fast and packed with traffic!

How much money can you make?

You can initially charge up to $5 per gig. Once you establish yourself and get some good reviews in, you will have the option to add-on extras to your gig and charge up to $65.

Why is this a reliable source of income?

Traffic, traffic, traffic! I get several fiverr gigs a day, almost too many, and I have NEVER promoted my services to anyone! If you get on fiverr, make a good profile page, descriptive gig page, and give it a few days. You will soon be getting those notifications to get to work!

Fiverr.com is an EXCELLENT way to explore your talents, find out what sort of work you love to do, and establish yourself as a professional and business-owner. There are unlimited gigs that you can offer, from singing "Happy Birthday" in a pink bunny suit, to offering customers a hilarious prank-call to their boss!

Step Nine

www.bluezebraappointmentsetting.com

Who can work here?

Any person 18 and older, who is professional and courteous on the phone and great with customers.

What is the job made up of?

This job is professional cold-calling and appointment setting from home. Bluezebra is a professional appointment-setting company, with many other businesses using their services.

How much money can you make?

$15-$25 per hour depending on skill level. Pretty darn good!

Why is this a reliable source of income?

Not only do they pay you your hourly rate, but they also offer incentives and bonuses, and they have on-going and consistent projects.

Step Ten

www.kdp.amazon.com

I did it, I saved the best for last.

Who can work for Amazon KDP?

KDP is literally around the world. Anyone with a computer and internet access can self-publish.

What is the job made up of?

Keep in mind that you do not need to be an author, or even a writer to profit from Amazon KDP. You can publish public domain content (over one-hundred years old) and as long as you add value to it, (example; pictures, additional info on a topic, any sort of new content) you can post it up and sell it. You can also publish short guides (such as this one), blogs, children's books, you name it. But if you are an author, and not on KDP yet, you're missing some great income!

How much money can you make?

This is up to you! The sky is the limit. Once you learn the system, which takes most about a year, you can position your content to reach the best audience and make the most sales. I have done very, very well with Amazon KDP.

Why is this a reliable source of income?

Not only is this source reliable, but 75% of eBook readers buy their content from Amazon. Also, once you work hard to finish a great novel, guide, story, etcetera, you never have to do that again, but you will always be paid for it...PASSIVE INCOME!

If you have a book online, or even if you are thinking about getting started with KDP, I highly suggest reading this book to learn about the small, yet important (and overlooked) tactics that WILL sell your book! The Psychology of Selling a Book Online will give you all the information you need to be successful when publishing.

Climb that Ladder!

I hope that you will *try* every one of these steps. I know that if you do, at least a couple of them will be permanent steps to the financial freedom and success that we all deserve. You can easily find your passion by implementing my ten steps as well as grow as a professional and learn the ropes of working-at home.

YOU WILL SEE RESULTS if you stick with it!

Good Luck, and thank you for reading my guide.

If you found this information helpful, please let me know by reviewing this book on Amazon. You can also find my other books on making money, by checking out my author profile below.

http://www.amazon.com/-/e/B00F292ALG